D1540419

"MAY I?"

by Janet Riehecky
illustrated by Gwen Connelly

GRAHAM PUBLIC LIBRARY, UNION GROVE, WI

Created by

THE
CHILD'S
WORLD

Distributed by CHILDRENS PRESS®
Chicago, Illinois

CHILDRENS PRESS HARDCOVER EDITION
ISBN 0-516-06247-6

CHILDRENS PRESS PAPERBACK EDITION
ISBN 0-516-46247-4

Library of Congress Cataloging in Publication Data

Riehecky, Janet, 1953-
    May I? / by Janet Riehecky ; illustrated by Gwen Connelly.
        p. cm. — (Manners matter)
    Summary: Describes various situations in which it is appropriate
to say, "May I?"
    ISBN 0-89565-388-5
    1. Etiquette for children and youth.   [1. Etiquette.]
I. Connelly, Gwen, ill.   II. Title.   III. Series.
BJ1857.C5R49   1989
395'.122—dc19   88-16838
                                                         CIP
                                                          AC

©1989 The Child's World, Inc.
Elgin, IL
All rights reserved. Printed in U.S.A.

1 2 3 4 5 6 7 8 9 10 11 12 R 97 96 95 94 93 92 91 90 89

"MAY I?"

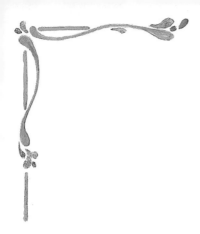

MANNERS MATTER all day through.
Say, "I'm sorry" or "I didn't mean to."

"Please" or "May I?" or "After you"
Will help you with what you want to do.

When you treat others with respect and care,
You'll find you have friends everywhere.

Say "May I?" if you want to . . .

take a cookie . . .

go outside . . .

change the television channel . . .

borrow a pencil from your
friend . . .

help build a tower . . .

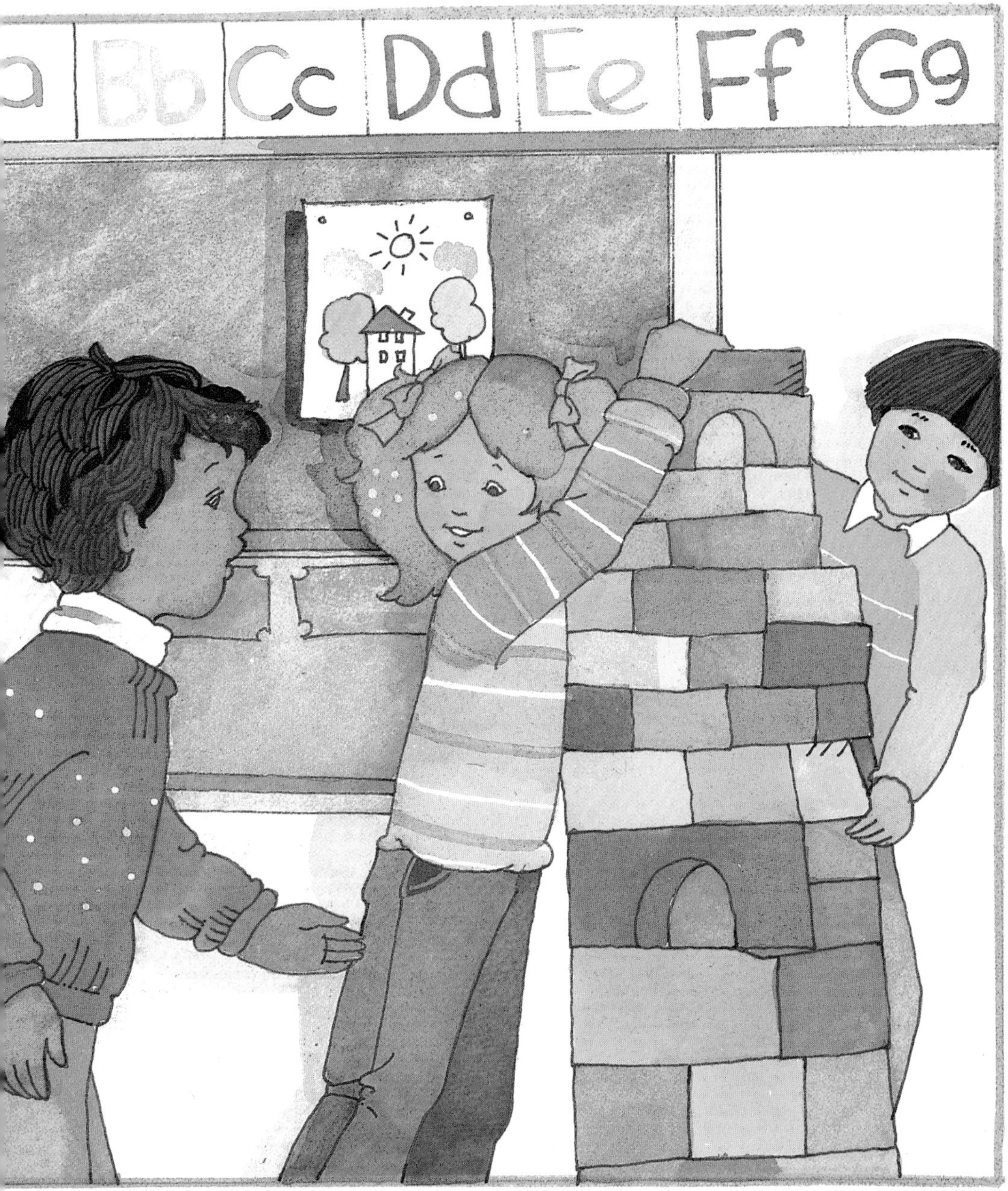
a Bb Cc Dd Ee Ff Gg

join in the game . . .

take a turn . . .

lick the bowl . . .

use your brother's mitt . . .

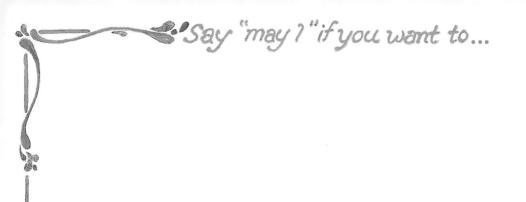

have a second helping . . .

move to the front . . .

have a treat . . .

choose a different book.

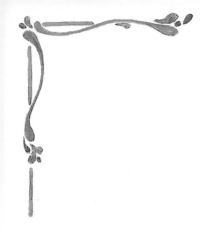

Say "May I?" when you want to do something or when you want to show consideration to others.